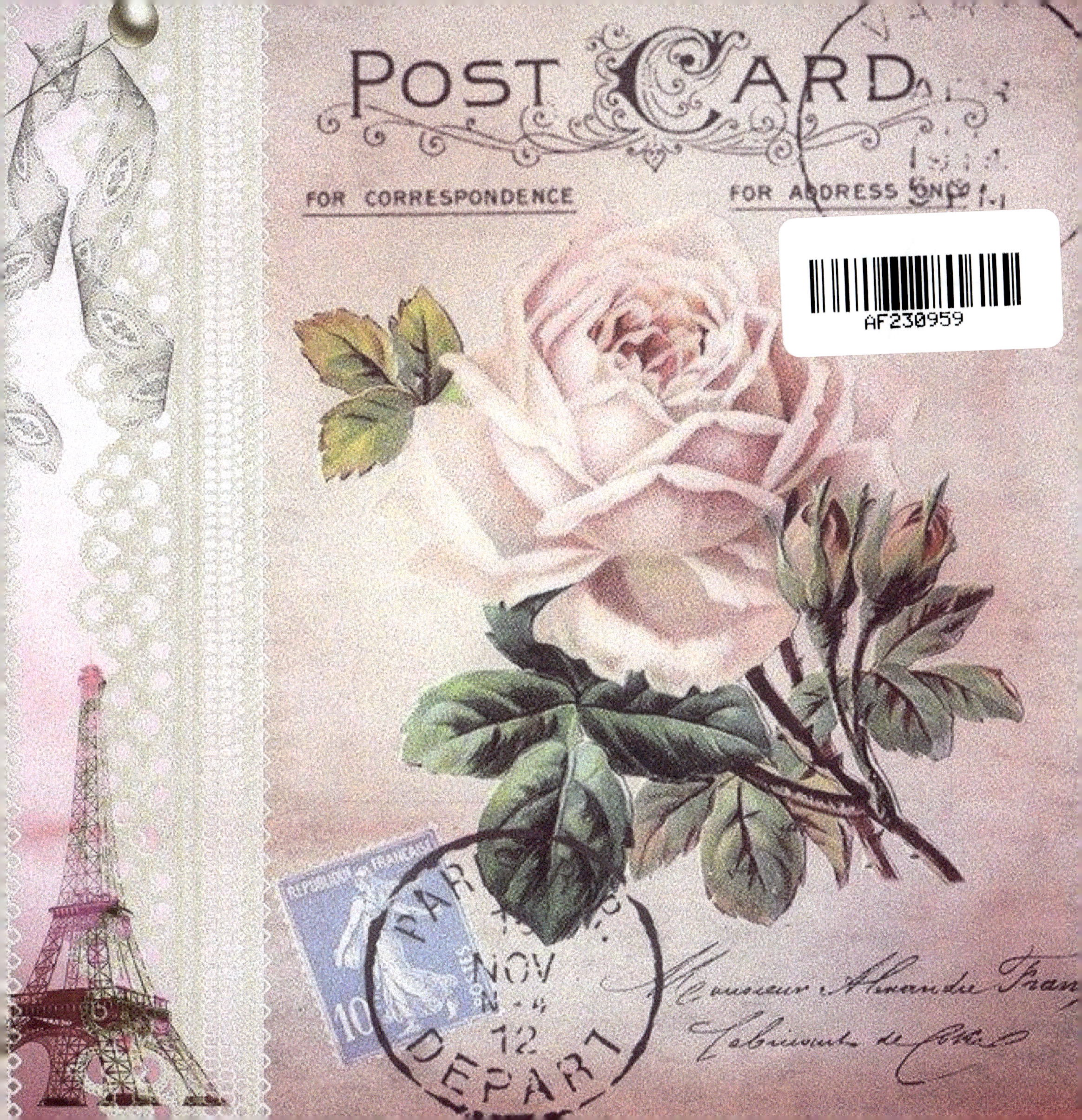
POST CARD
FOR CORRESPONDENCE
FOR ADDRESS ONLY
AF230959
RÉPUBLIQUE FRANÇAISE
PARIS
NOV
12
DEPART

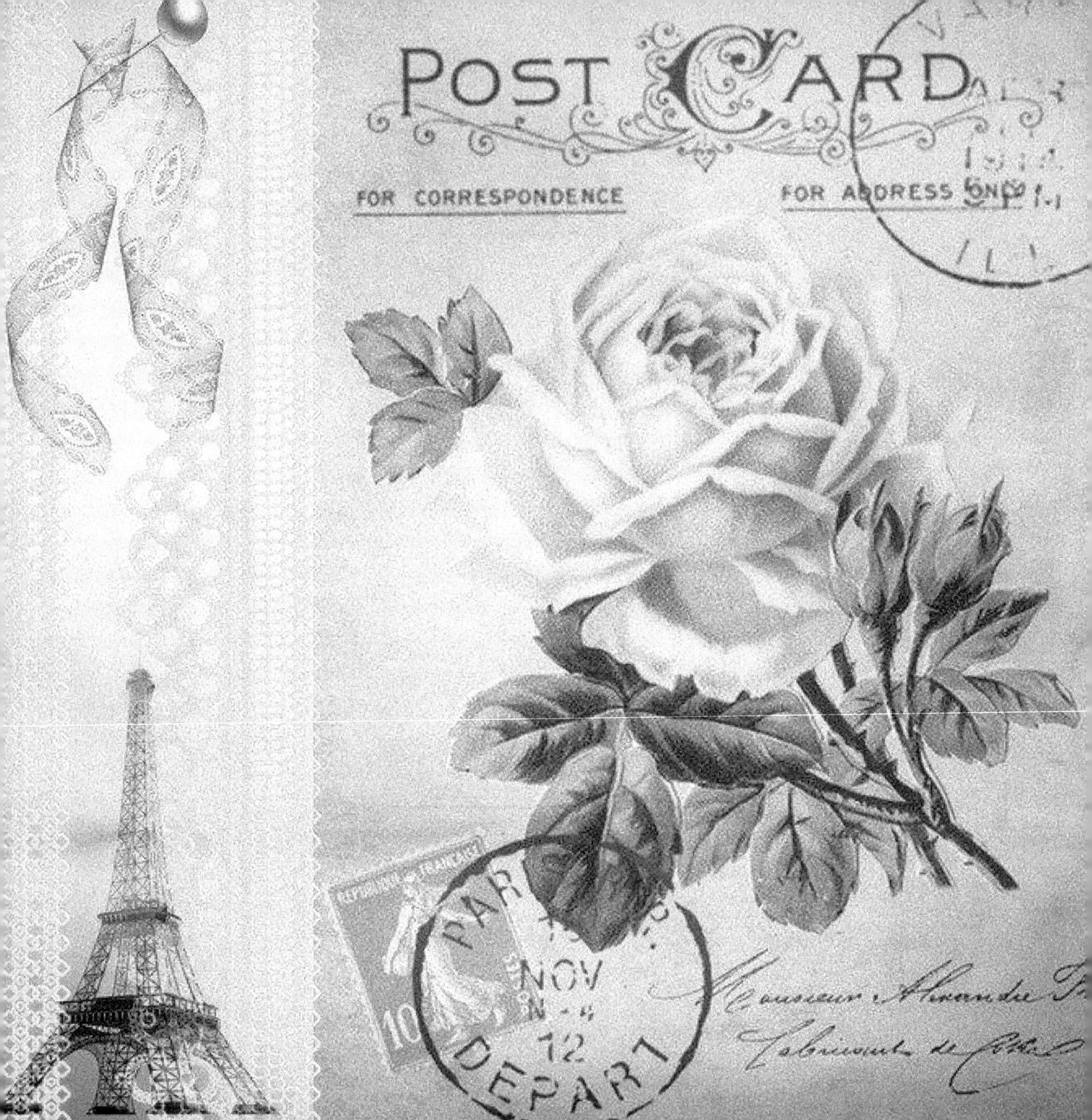
POST CARD
FOR CORRESPONDENCE
FOR ADDRESS ONLY
REPUBLIQUE FRANÇAISE
10
PARIS
NOV
12
DEPART

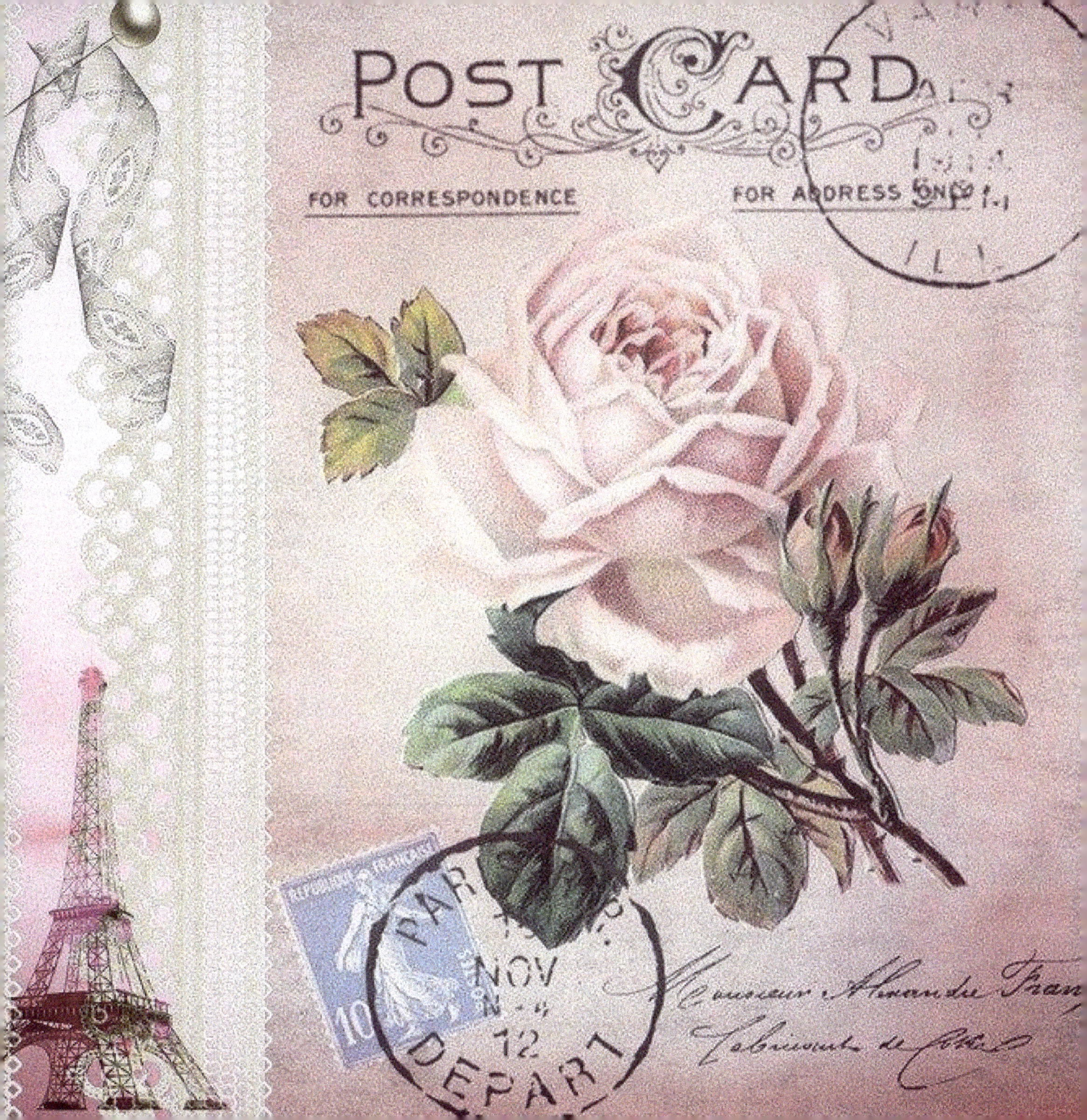
POST CARD
FOR CORRESPONDENCE
FOR ADDRESS ONLY

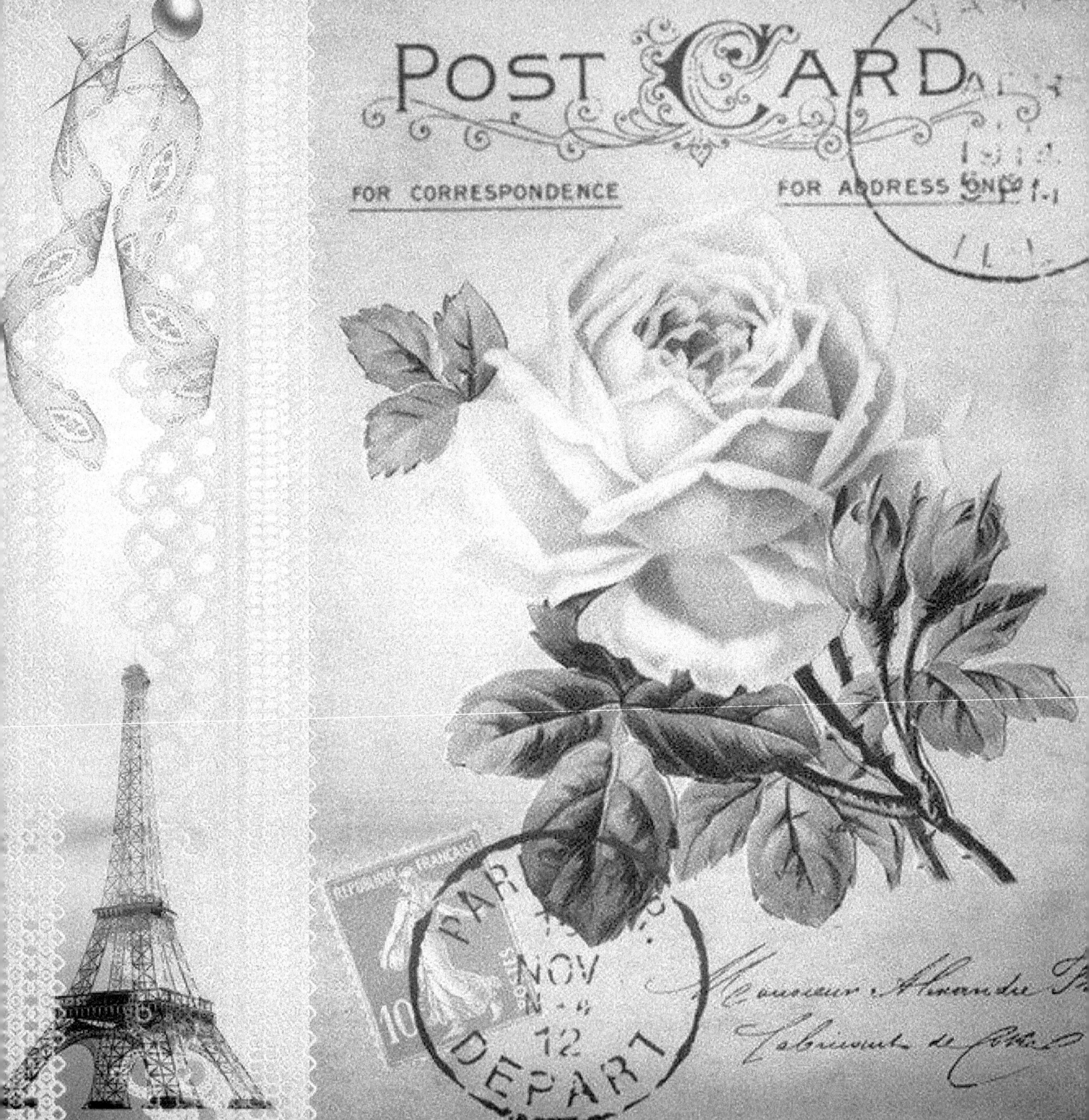

POST CARD
FOR CORRESPONDENCE
FOR ADDRESS ONLY
REPUBLIQUE FRANÇAISE
NOV
12
DEPART
PARIS

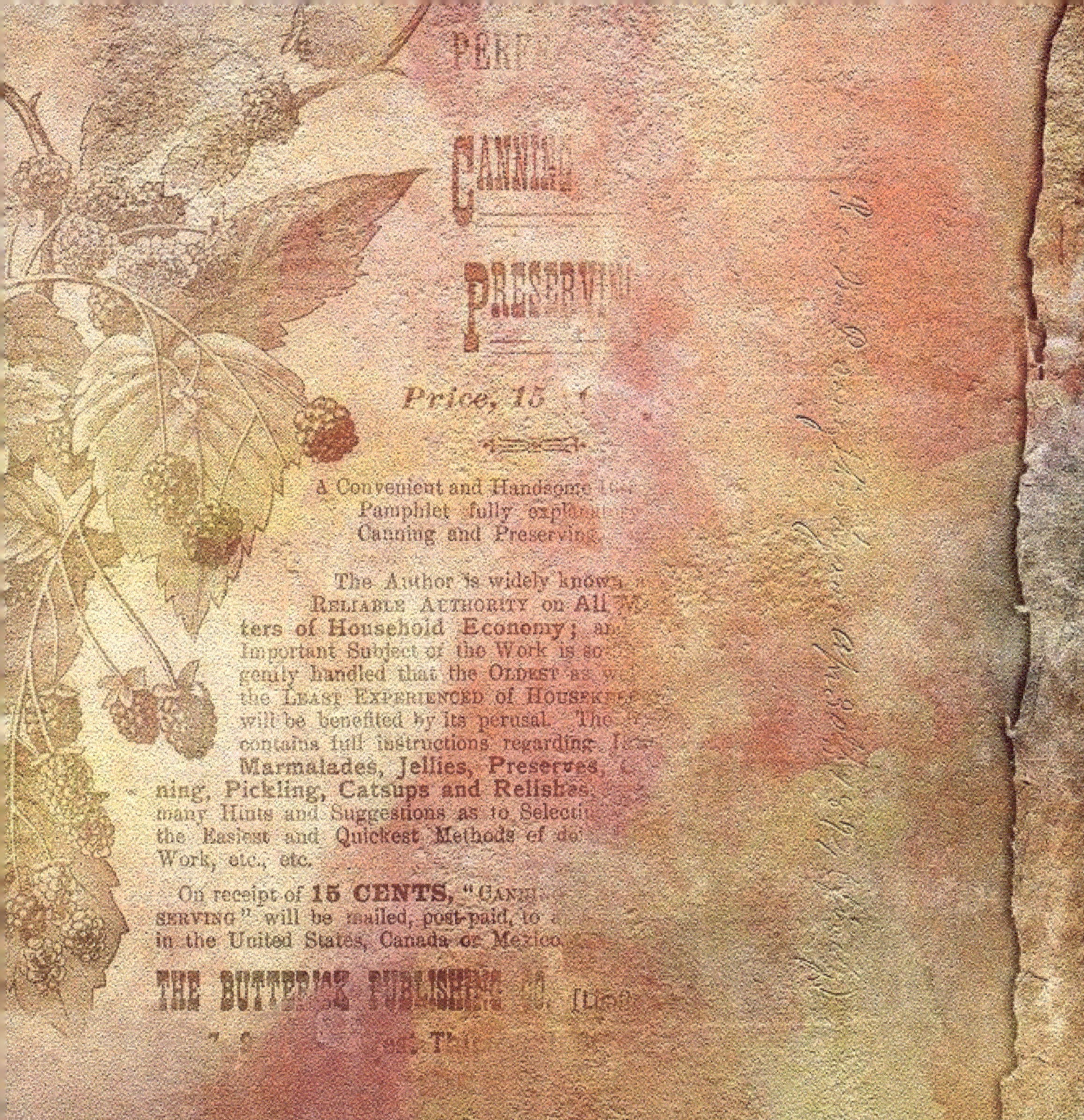

CANNING
PRESERVING

Price, 15

A Convenient and Handsome
Pamphlet fully explaining
Canning and Preserving.

The Author is widely known
RELIABLE AUTHORITY on All
ters of Household Economy; an
Important Subject of the Work is so
gently handled that the OLDEST as w
the LEAST EXPERIENCED of HOUSEKE
will be benefited by its perusal. The
contains full instructions regarding
Marmalades, Jellies, Preserves,
ning, Pickling, Catsups and Relishes
many Hints and Suggestions as to Selecti
the Easiest and Quickest Methods of do
Work, etc., etc.

On receipt of 15 CENTS, "CANN
SERVING" will be mailed, post-paid, to
in the United States, Canada or Mexico.

THE BUTTERICK PUBLISHING CO. [Limit

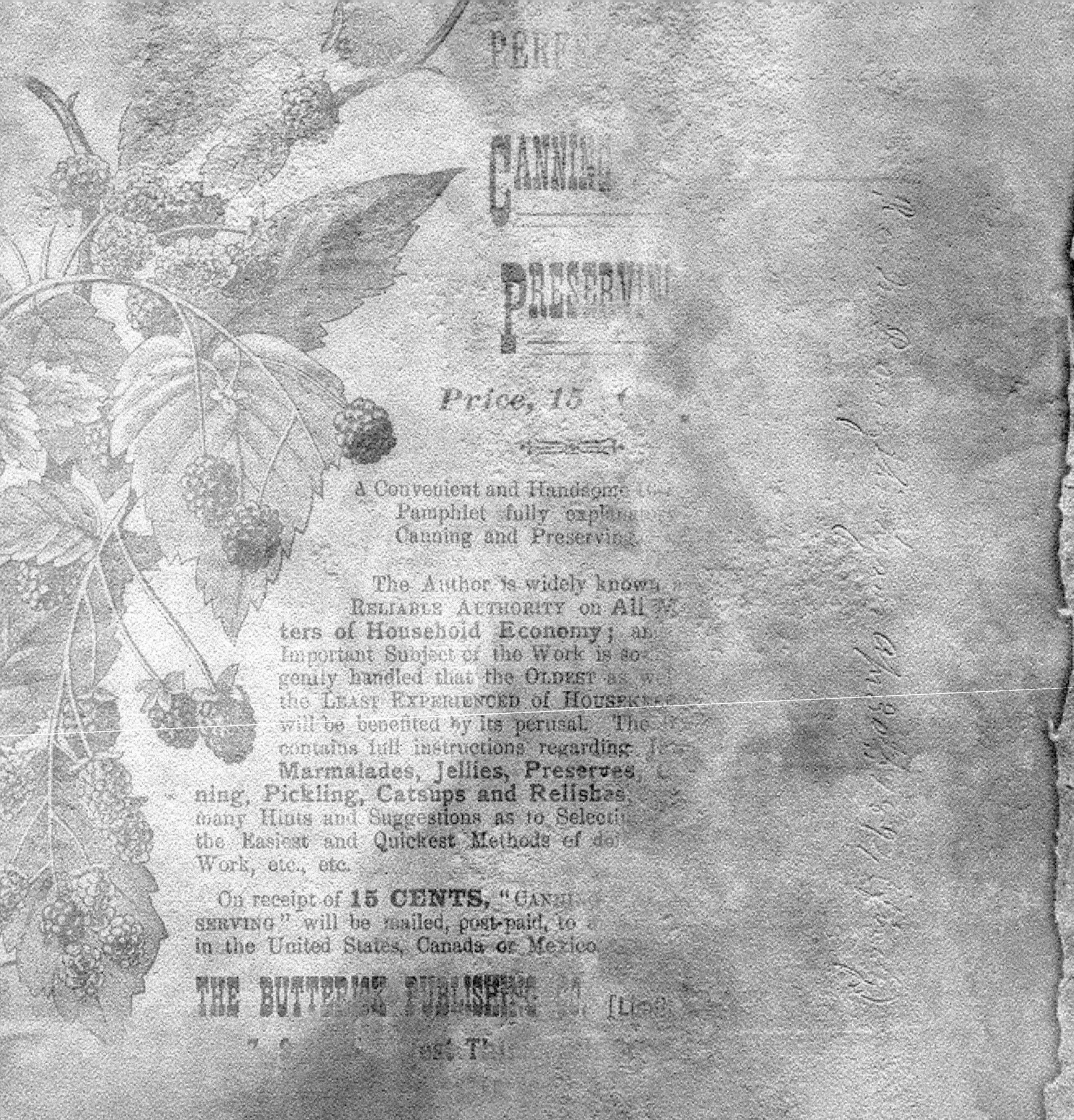

PERFECT

CANNING

AND

PRESERVING

Price, 15 Cents

A Convenient and Handsome Little
Pamphlet fully explaining
Canning and Preserving

The Author is widely known as a
RELIABLE AUTHORITY on All Mat-
ters of Household Economy; and the
Important Subject of the Work is so
gently handled that the OLDEST as well as
the LEAST EXPERIENCED of HOUSEKEEPERS
will be benefited by its perusal. The Work
contains full instructions regarding Jams,
Marmalades, Jellies, Preserves, Canning, Pickling, Catsups and Relishes,
many Hints and Suggestions as to Selecting
the Easiest and Quickest Methods of doing
Work, etc., etc.

On receipt of 15 CENTS, "CANNING AND PRE-
SERVING" will be mailed, post-paid, to any Address
in the United States, Canada or Mexico.

THE BUTTERICK PUBLISHING CO. [Limited]

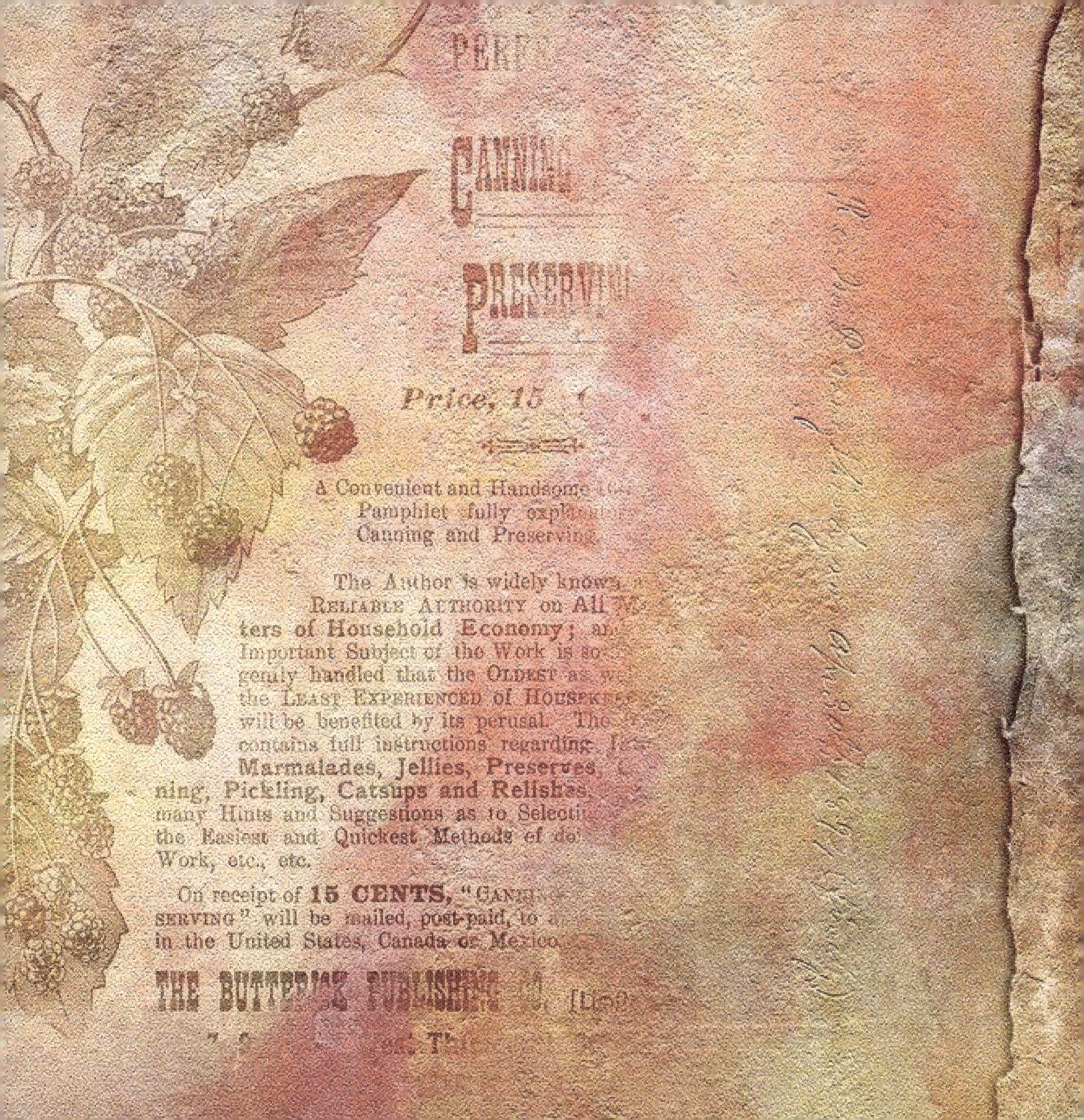

PERFECT
CANNING
and PRESERVING

Price, 15 cents

A Convenient and Handsome Little
Pamphlet fully explaining
Canning and Preserving.

The Author is widely known as
Reliable Authority on All Mat-
ters of Household Economy; and the
Important Subject of the Work is so
gently handled that the Oldest as well as
the Least Experienced of Housekeepers
will be benefited by its perusal. The book
contains full instructions regarding Jams,
Marmalades, Jellies, Preserves, Canning, Pickling, Catsups and Relishes, with
many Hints and Suggestions as to Selecting
the Easiest and Quickest Methods of doing
Work, etc., etc.

On receipt of 15 CENTS, "Canning and Preserving" will be mailed, post-paid, to any address
in the United States, Canada or Mexico.

THE BUTTERICK PUBLISHING CO. [Limited]

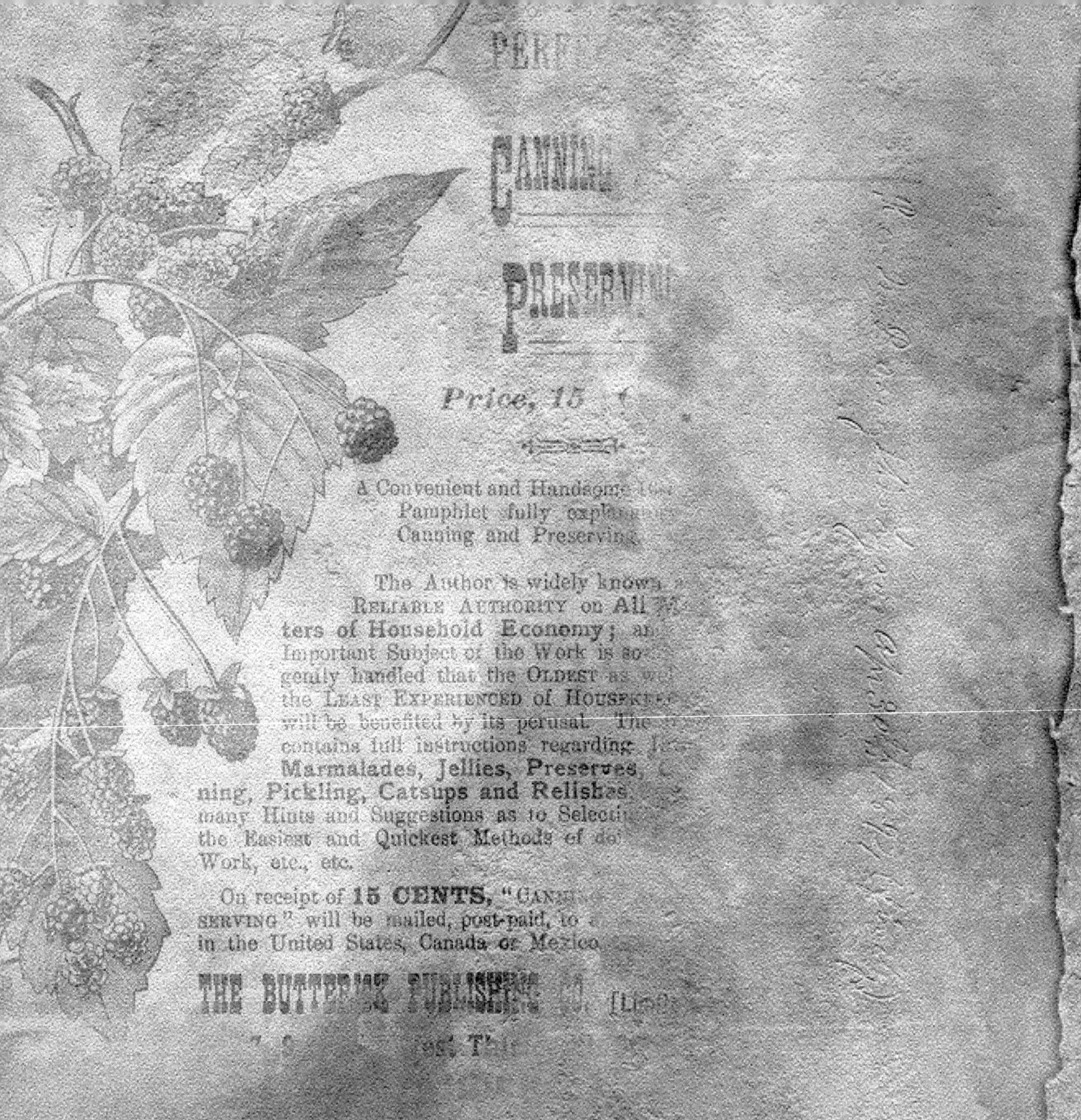

Dover Dunkirk Brussels Aix la Chapelle

North Sea

Zuyder Zee Utrecht

NETHERLANDS Rhine

London Dover

Dunkirk

Brussels Aix la Chapelle

Waterloo

Ramillies

GERMANY

Metz

LORRAINE

Nancy

ENGLAND

L. Constance

Sempach

SWITZERLAND

L. Geneva

Nantes

FRANCE

AND THE

NEIGHBORING

COUNTRIES

46

16

ITALY

S P A I N

Roncesvalles

1 Long. West   0   Long. East 4 from London   8

Marsan

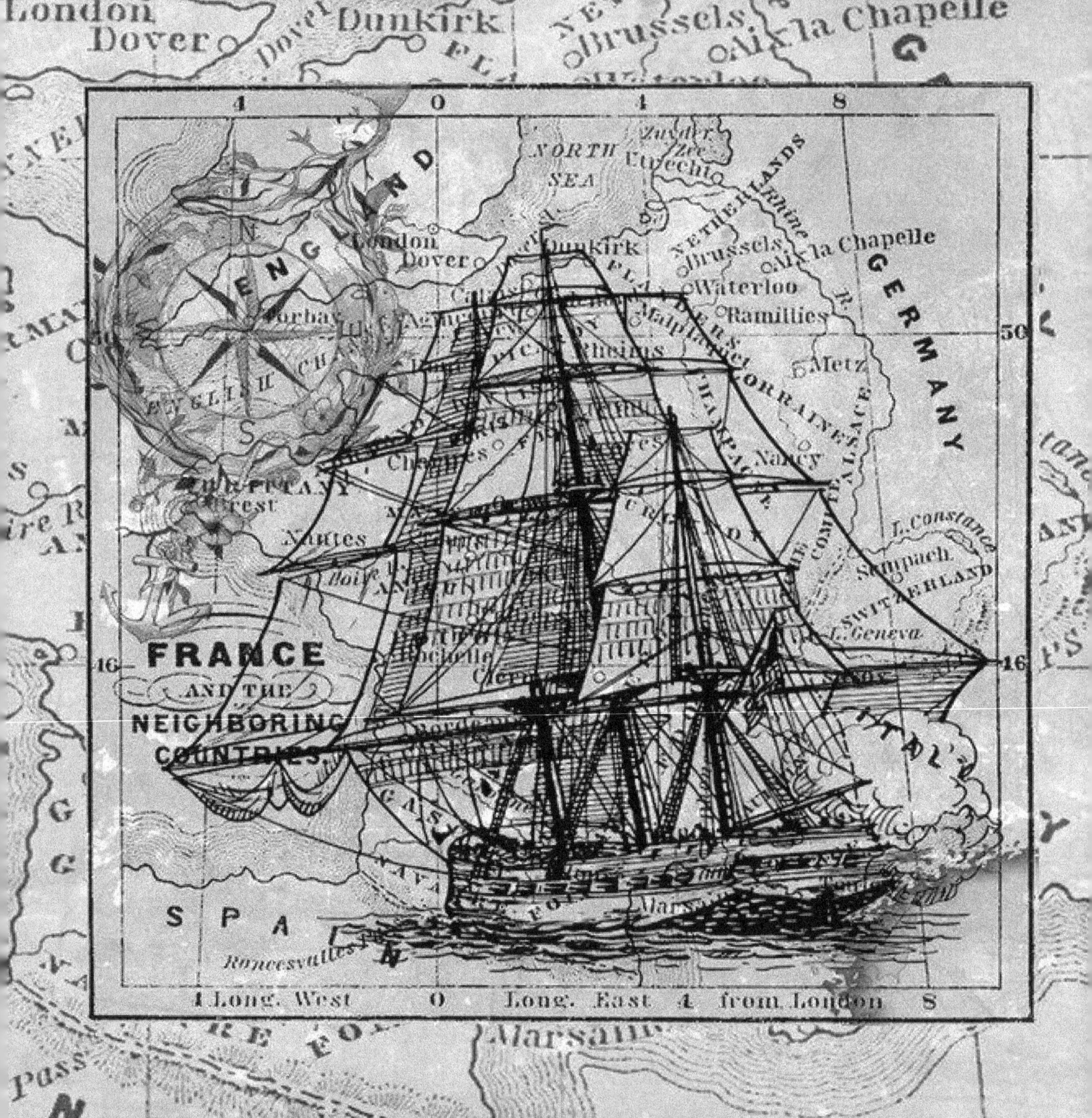
London
Dover
Dunkirk
Brussels
Aix la Chapelle
NORTH SEA
Zuyder Zee
Utrecht
NETHERLANDS
GERMANY
Brussels
Aix la Chapelle
Waterloo
Ramillies
Metz
LORRAINE
Nancy
ALSACE
L. Constance
Sempach
SWITZERLAND
L. Geneva
ENGLAND
London
Dover
ENGLISH CHANNEL
Torbay
BRITTANY
Brest
Nantes
FRANCE
AND THE
NEIGHBORING
COUNTRIES
Rheims
ITALY
SPAIN
Roncesvalles
GASCONY
Marseilles
Long. West
Long. East
from London

Dover Dunkirk Brussels Aix la Chapelle

ENGLAND

London
Dover

NORTH SEA

Zuyder Zee Utrecht

NETHERLANDS

Brussels Aix la Chapelle
Waterloo
Ramillies

GERMANY

Metz

LORRAINE

Nancy

ALSACE

L. Constance
Sempach

SWITZERLAND

L. Geneva

FRANCE
AND THE
NEIGHBORING
COUNTRIES

Nantes
Loire

BRITTANY

ITALY

SPAIN

Roncesvalles

Marsala

4 Long. West   0   Long. East   4   from London   8

London
Dover
Dunkirk
Brussels
Aix la Chapelle
Waterloo

ENGLAND
London
Dover
NORTH SEA
Zuyder Zee
Utrecht
NETHERLANDS
Brussels
Aix la Chapelle
Waterloo
Ramillies
GERMANY
Metz
LORRAINE
ALSACE
Nancy
L. Constance
Sempach
SWITZERLAND
L. Geneva
ENGLISH CH.
Torbay
BRITTANY
Brest
Nantes
Loire

FRANCE
AND THE
**NEIGHBORING
COUNTRIES**

46
16
50

ITALY

S P A I N
Roncesvalles

4 Long. West   0   Long. East   4   from London   8

Marseilles

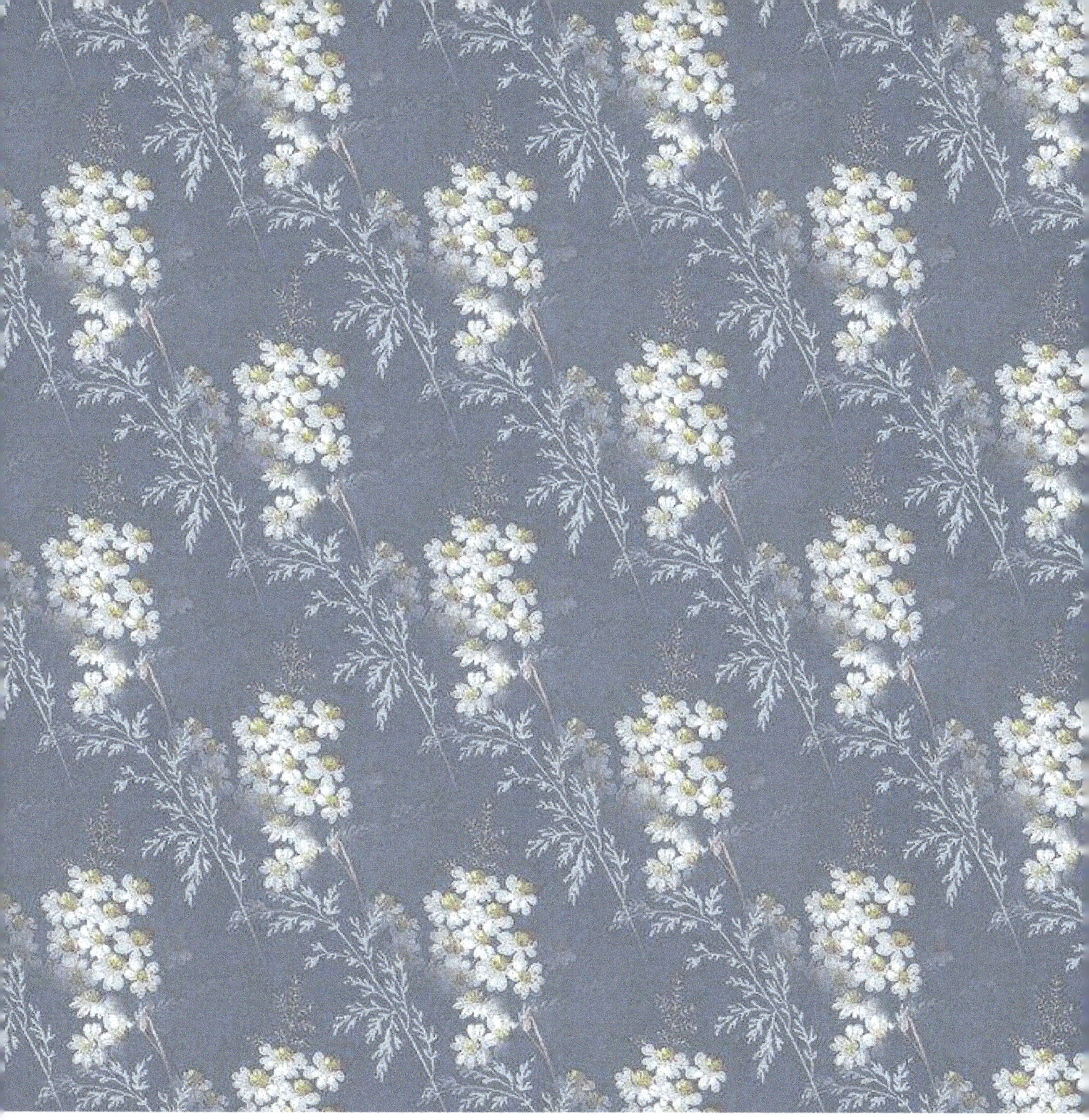

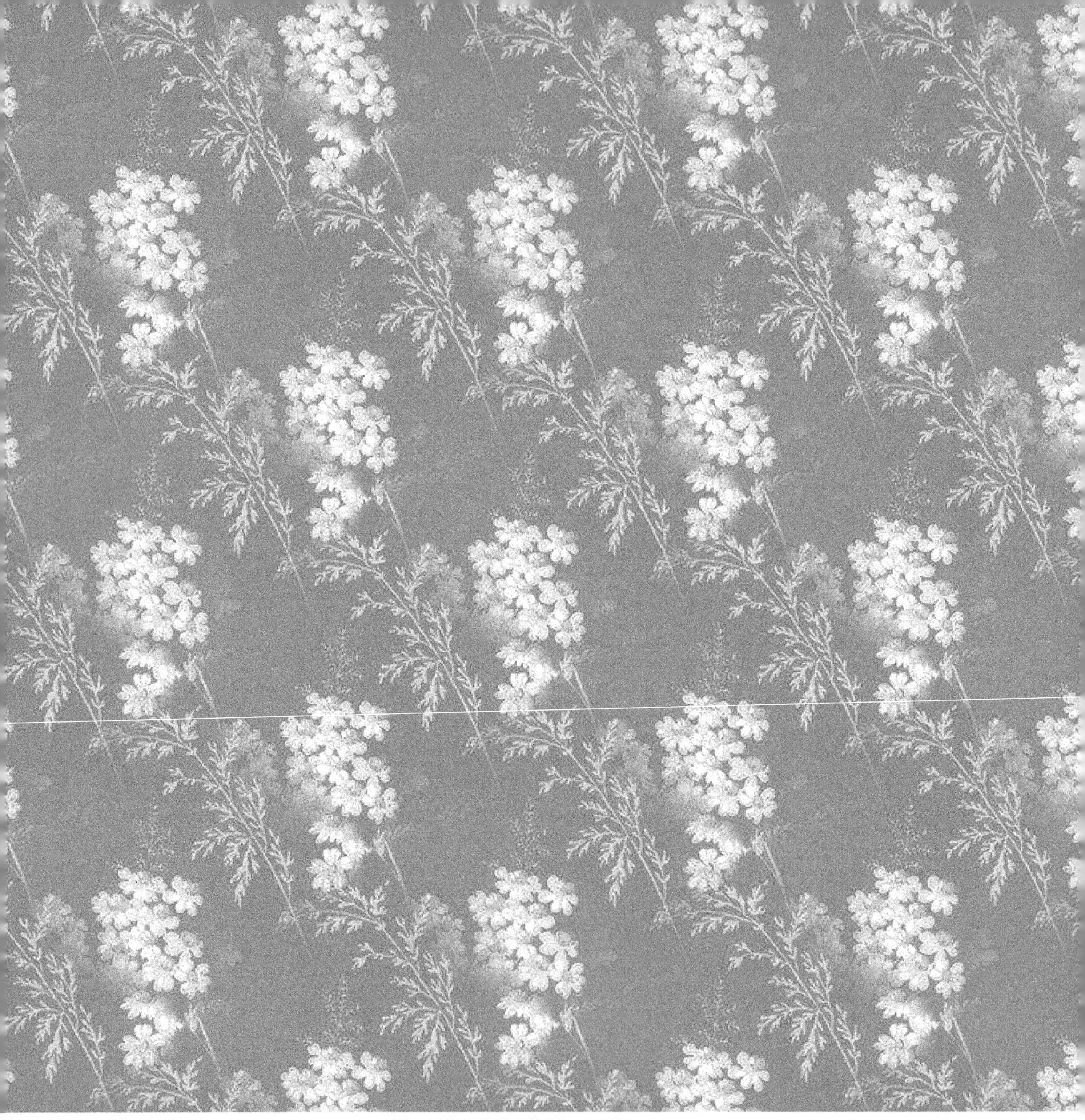

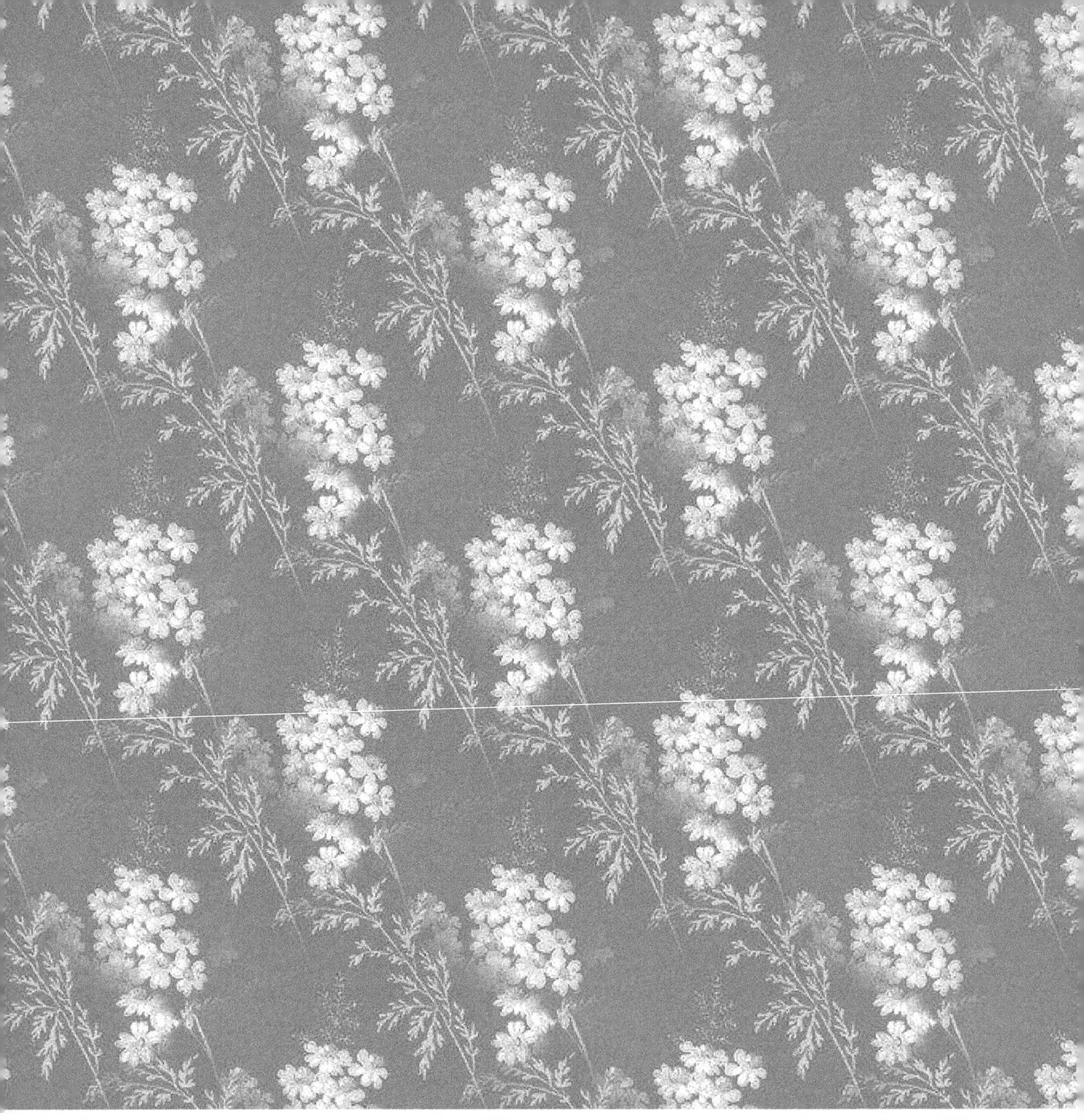

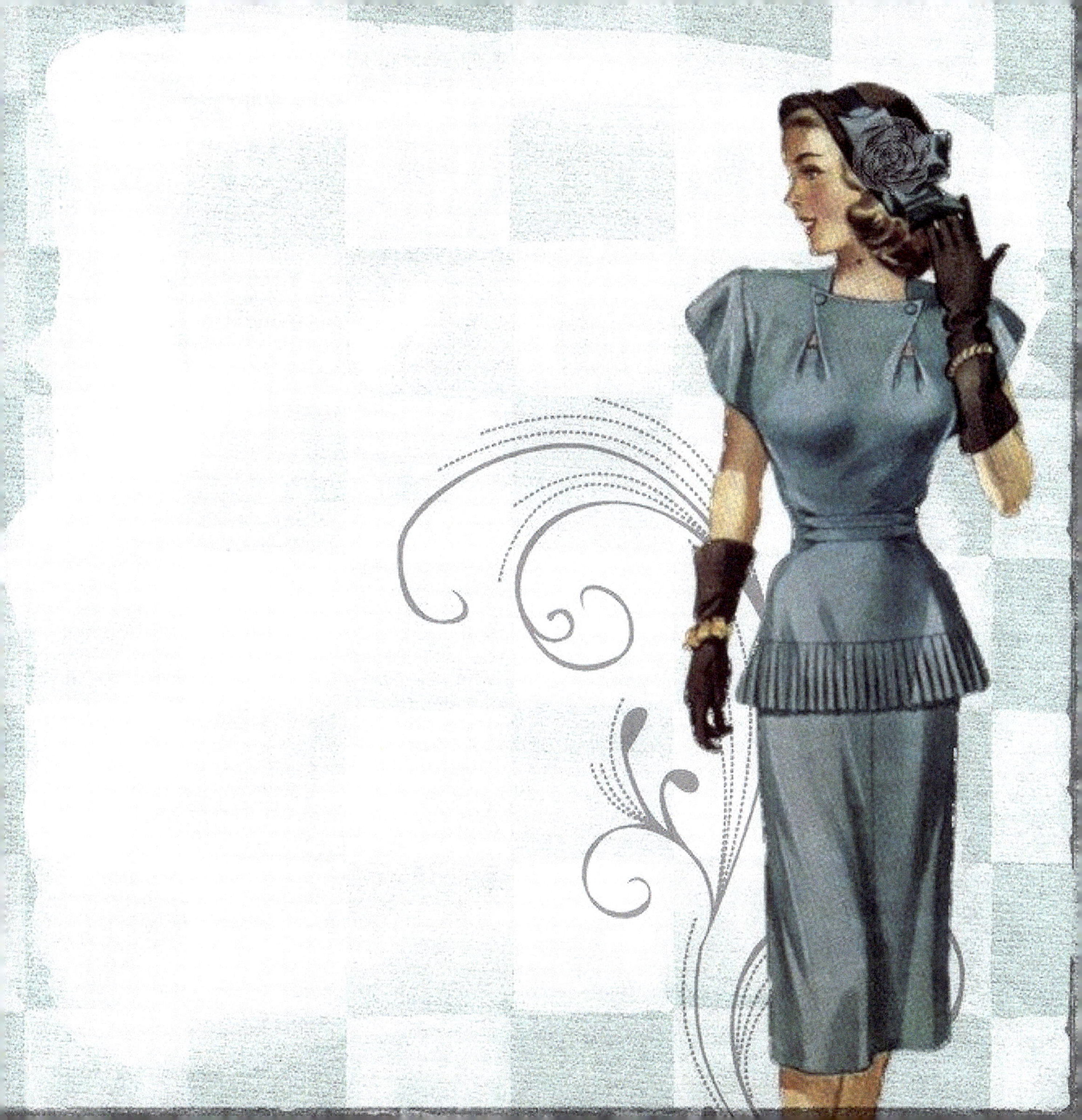

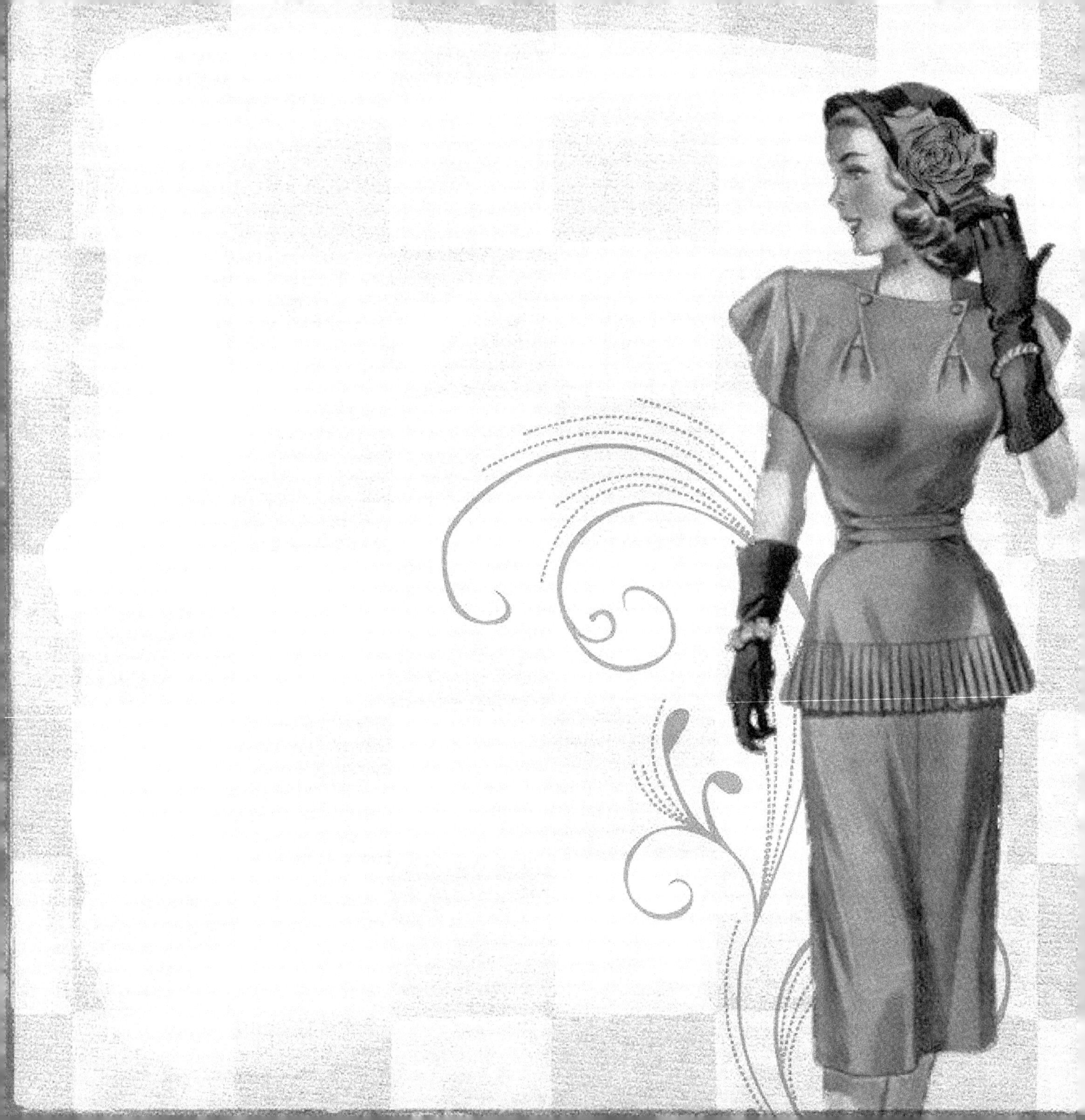

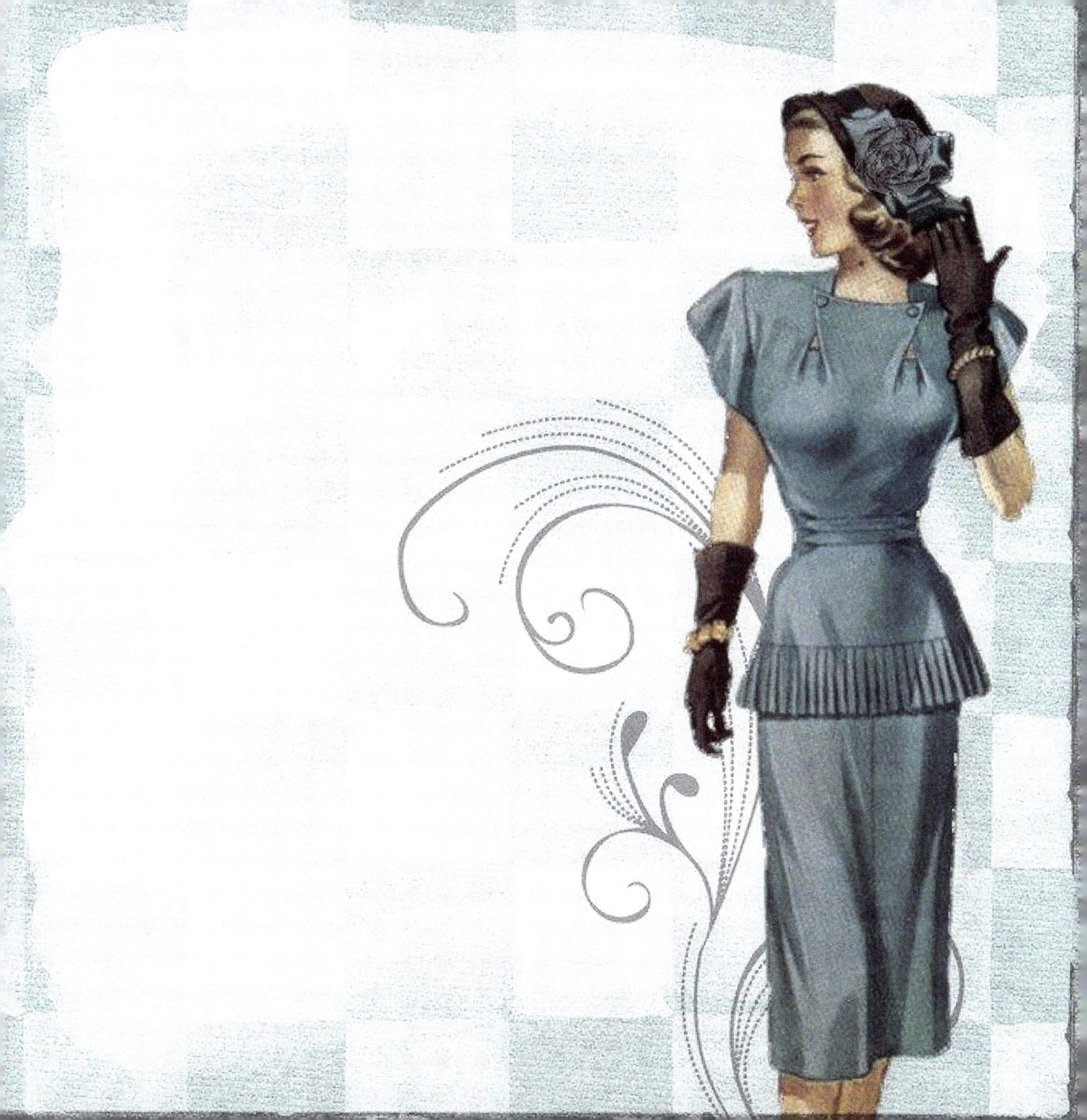

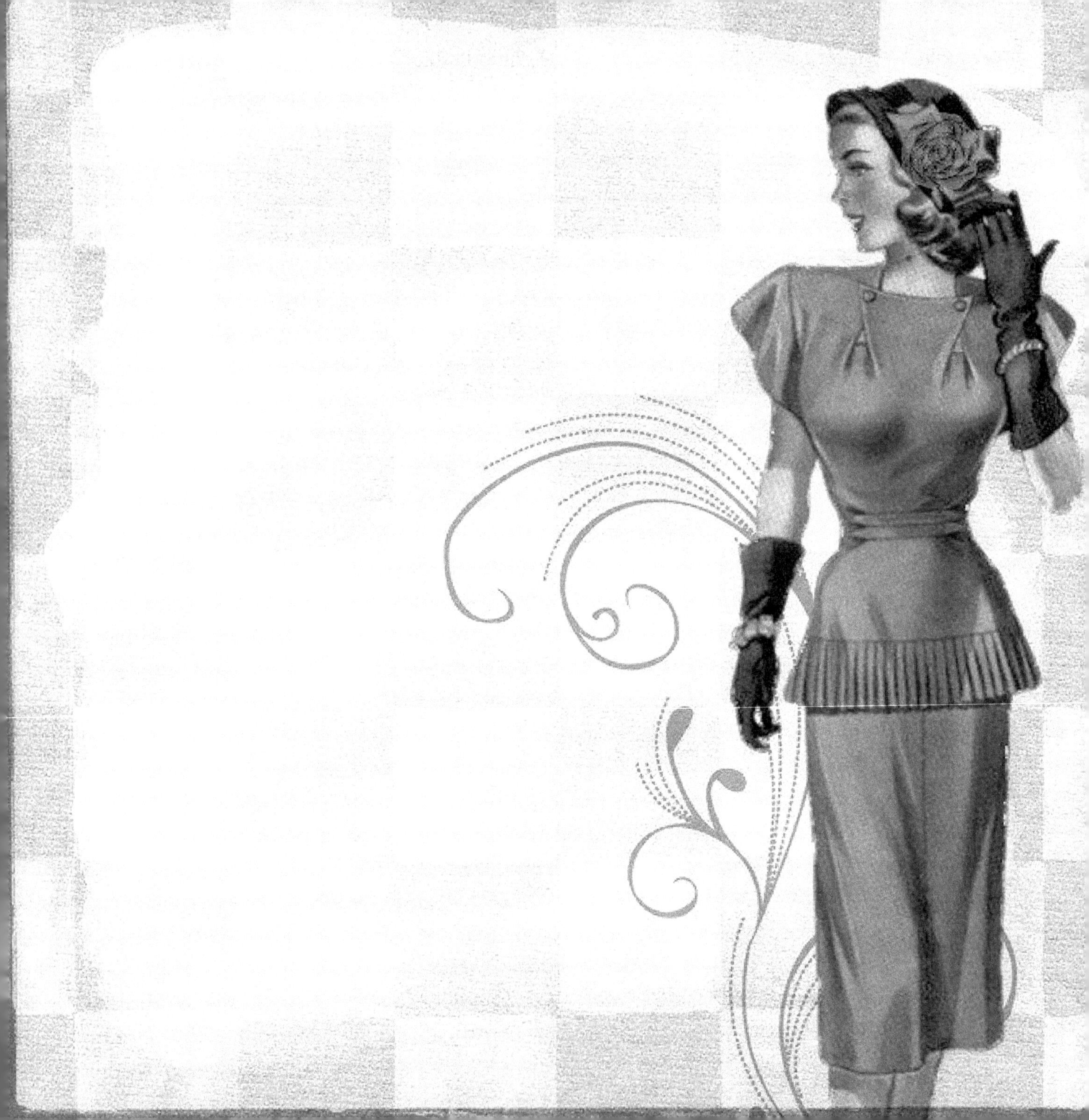

9 781951 373207